How to Draw a Self Portrait for Kids

Step-By-Step Portraiture Instructions, Features of The Face, Capturing Emotions and More

Copyright © 2021

All rights reserved.

DEDICATION

The author and publisher have provided this e-book to you for your personal use only. You may not make this e-book publicly available in any way. Copyright infringement is against the law. If you believe the copy of this e-book you are reading infringes on the author's copyright, please notify the publisher at: https://us.macmillan.com/piracy

Contents

Portrait 1

How to Draw a Portrait 5

How to Capture Emotion in Portrait Photography 14

Shading Techniques 27

Techniques For Highlighting 39

How to Take a Good Selfie 42

Creative Self Portrait Ideas for Photographers 49

Portrait

A portrait is a painting, photograph, sculpture, or other artistic representation of a person, in which the face and its expression is predominant. The intent is to display the likeness, personality, and even the mood of the person. For this reason, in photography a portrait is generally not a snapshot, but a composed image of a person in a still position. A portrait often shows a person looking directly at the painter or photographer, in order to most successfully engage the subject with the viewer.

History

Prehistorical portraiture

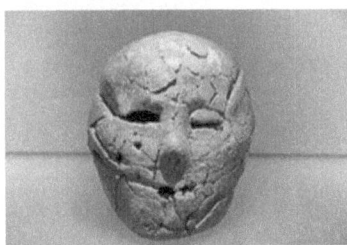

Plastered skull, Tell es-Sultan, Jericho, Pre-Pottery Neolithic B, circa 9000 BC

Plastered human skulls were reconstructed human skulls that were made in the ancient Levant between 9000 and 6000 BC in the Pre-Pottery Neolithic B period. They represent some of the oldest forms of art in the Middle East and demonstrate that the prehistoric population took great care in burying their ancestors below their homes. The skulls denote some of the earliest sculptural examples of portraiture in the history of art.[3]

Historical portraiture

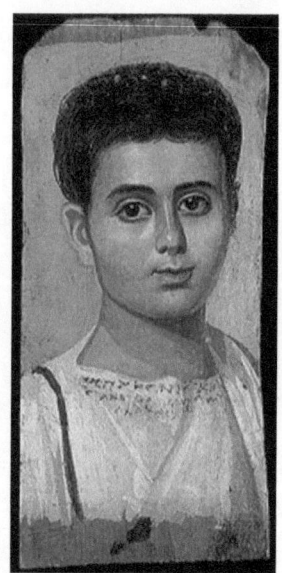

Roman-Egyptian funeral portrait of a young boy

Most early representations that are clearly intended to show an individual are of rulers, and tend to follow idealizing artistic conventions, rather than the individual features of the subject's body, though when there is no other evidence as to the ruler's appearance the degree of idealization can be hard to assess. Nonetheless, many

Portrait for Kids

subjects, such as Akhenaten and some other Egyptian pharaohs, can be recognised by their distinctive features. The 28 surviving rather small statues of Gudea, ruler of Lagash in Sumeria between c. 2144–2124 BC, show a consistent appearance with some individuality, although it is sometimes disputed that these count as portraits.[4]

Some of the earliest surviving painted portraits of people who were not rulers are the Greco-Roman funeral portraits that survived in the dry climate of Egypt's Fayum district. These are almost the only paintings from the classical world that have survived, apart from frescos, though many sculptures and portraits on coins have fared better. Although the appearance of the figures differs considerably, they are considerably idealized, and all show relatively young people, making it uncertain whether they were painted from life.

The art of the portrait flourished in Ancient Greek and especially Roman sculpture, where sitters demanded individualized and realistic portraits, even unflattering ones. During the 4th century, the portrait began to retreat in favor of an idealized symbol of what that person looked like. (Compare the portraits of Roman Emperors Constantine I and Theodosius I at their entries.) In the Europe of the Early Middle

Portrait for Kids

Ages representations of individuals are mostly generalized. True portraits of the outward appearance of individuals re-emerged in the late Middle Ages, in tomb monuments, donor portraits, miniatures in illuminated manuscripts and then panel paintings.

Moche ceramic portrait. Larco Museum Collection. Lima-Peru

Moche culture of Peru was one of the few ancient civilizations which produced portraits. These works accurately represent anatomical features in great detail. The individuals portrayed would have been recognizable without the need for other symbols or a written reference to their names. The individuals portrayed were members of the ruling elite, priests, warriors and even distinguished artisans.[5] They were represented during several stages of their lives. The faces of gods were also depicted. To date, no portraits of women have been found. There is particular emphasis on the representation of the details of headdresses, hairstyles, body adornment and face painting.

One of the best-known portraits in the Western world is Leonardo da Vinci's painting titled Mona Lisa, which is a painting of Lisa del Giocondo. What has been claimed as the world's oldest known portrait was found in 2006 in the Vilhonneur grotto near Angoulême and is thought to be 27,000 years old.

Portrait for Kids

How to Draw a Portrait

Method 1

A Realistic Female Human PortraitDownload Article

1. Draw a circle for the head.

2. Draw two lines from the left and right sides, which meet and form an open triangle.

3. Draw a curve line connecting the ends from the circle to the tip below.

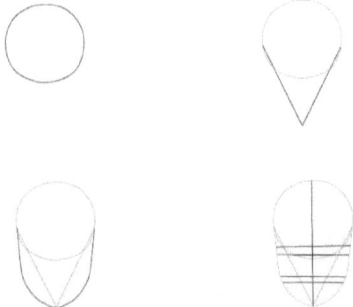

4. Draw a vertical line which divides the figures to halves. Draw two sets of parallel lines at the lower part of the circle.

5. Using the lines as guide, draw details for the eyes, eyebrows, nose, and mouth at their appropriate positions.

6. Trace the border lines.

7. Draw details for the woman's hair, neck, and shoulders – use curve

lines.

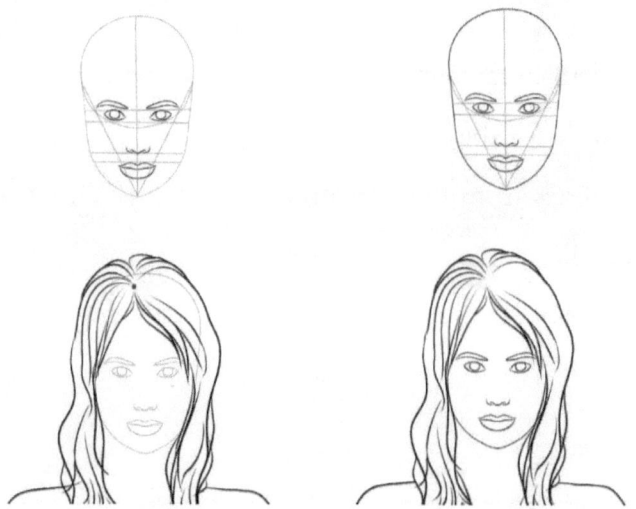

8. Trace with a pen and erase unnecessary lines.

9. Color to your liking!

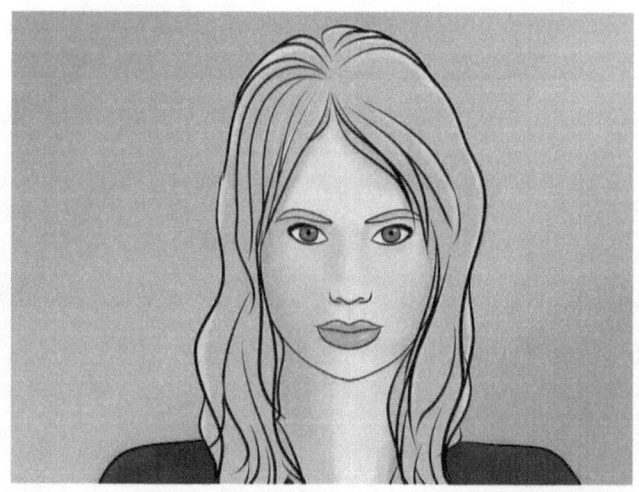

Portrait for Kids

Method 2

A Realistic Male Human PortraitDownload Article

1. Draw a circle for the head.

2. Draw a vertical lines in the middle which extends outside the circle. Draw a horizontal line inside the circle at the lower part. Draw two parallel lines of different lengths below the circle.

3. Draw a triangle using the ends from the sides of the circle and the tip of the middle line as vertices.

4. Draw curve lines which connect the circle to the tip of the triangle. the circle.

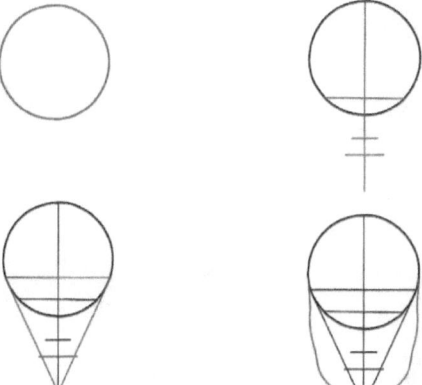

5. Draw a small triangle in the middle and draw the ears using curve lines.

Portrait for Kids

6. Using the lines as guide, draw details for the eyes, eyebrows, and mouth at their appropriate positions.

7. Refine the small triangle to resemble a nose and add details.

8. Trace with a pencil and erase unnecessary lines. Draw details for the hair and neck.

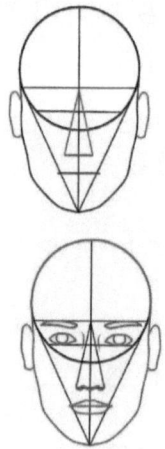
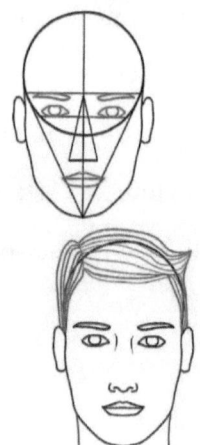

9. Erase unnecessary lines.

10. Color to your liking!

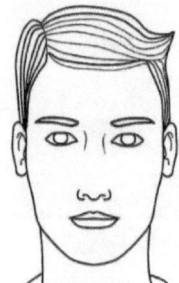
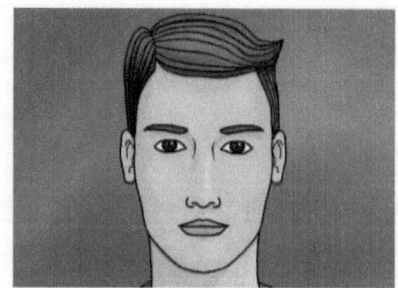

Portrait for Kids

Method 3

A Cartoon-like Human Female PortraitDownload Article

1.Draw a big vertical oval.

2.Bisect it with a vertical line and join a horizontal line across the the vertical line touching the edges of the oval for the guides to the eyes and nose.

3.Place a couple of short lines for the nose and mouth.

4.Add a small horizontal oval each on either side of the head for the ears.

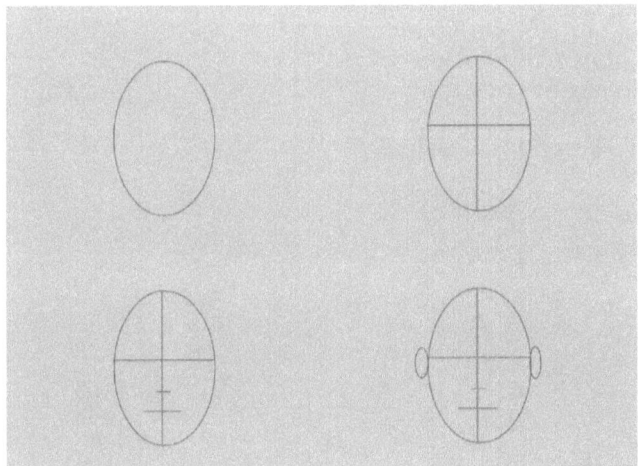

5.Put in symmetrical lines for the eyebrows.

6.Create leaf-like shapes each on either side for the eye-shapes.

7.Make lip-guides by joining a triangle on top with three lines at the

Portrait for Kids

bottom.

8. Create eye-balls within the eye-shapes.

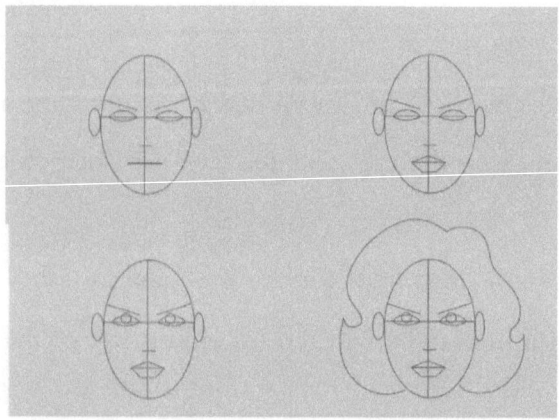

9. Draw the hair shape-outline.

10. On the basis of the guides, draw details of the portrait.

11. Erase all sketchy guide lines.

12. Color the pretty portrait.

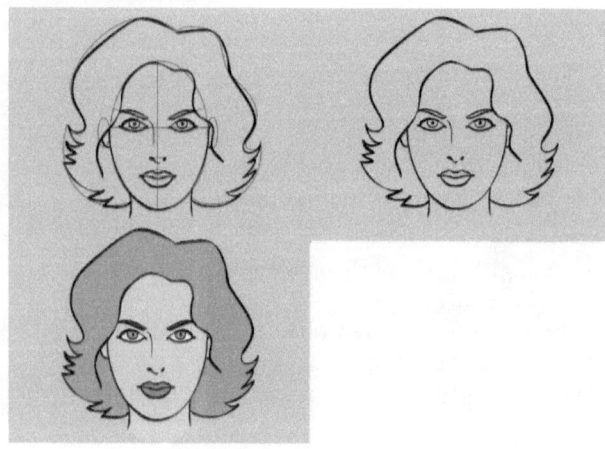

Portrait for Kids

Method 4

A Cartoon-like Human Male PortraitDownload Article

1. Make an oval.
2. Bisect it with a vertical line stretching out of the circle. Draw another horizontal line off–center touching the edges of the left and right edges of the oval.
3. Put two more horizontal lines at the bottom, one smaller than the other for the jaw and chin.
4. Join the jaw and chin guides with straight lines.

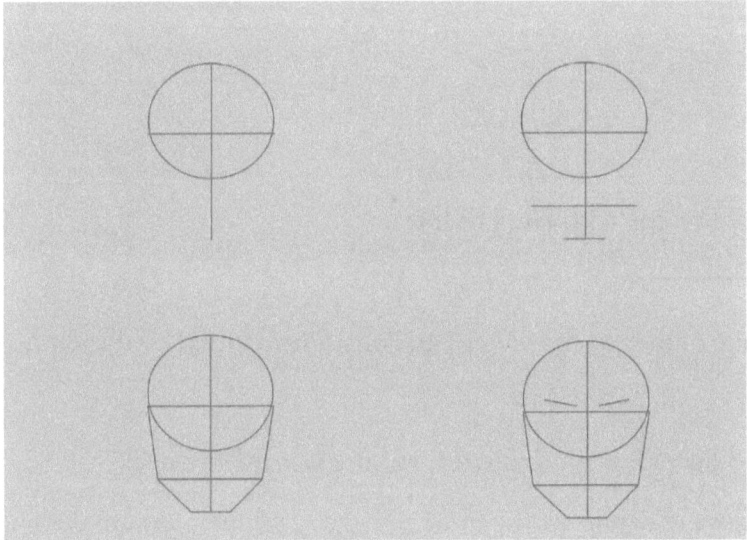

5. Make two symmetrical lines for the eyebrows.
6. Then make a triangle for the nose.

Portrait for Kids

7. Join an inverted triangle at the bottom of it.

8. Create a short horizontal line just below the nose for the mouth.

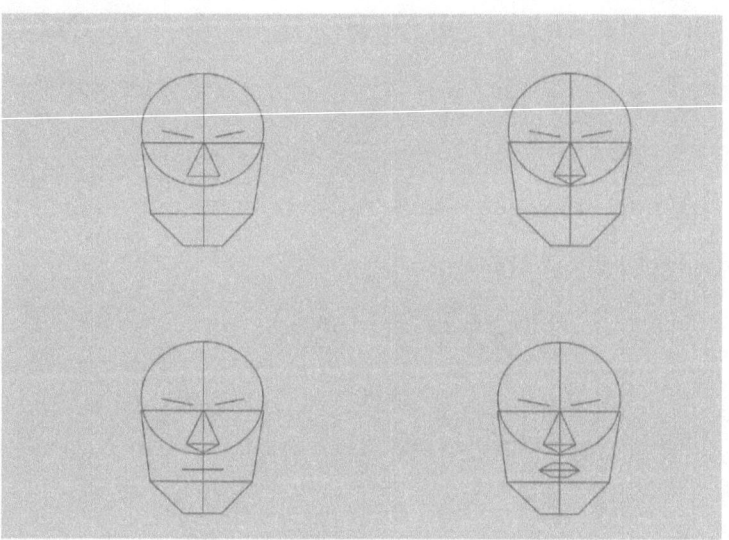

9. Make the lips with straight lines.

10. Draw the eyes' guide areas.

11. Make guides to the ears by making a horizontal oval each on either side.

12. Add lines dropping down from the jaw for the neck.

13. Draw the details of the male portrait. Follow it with making a guide for the hair.

Portrait for Kids

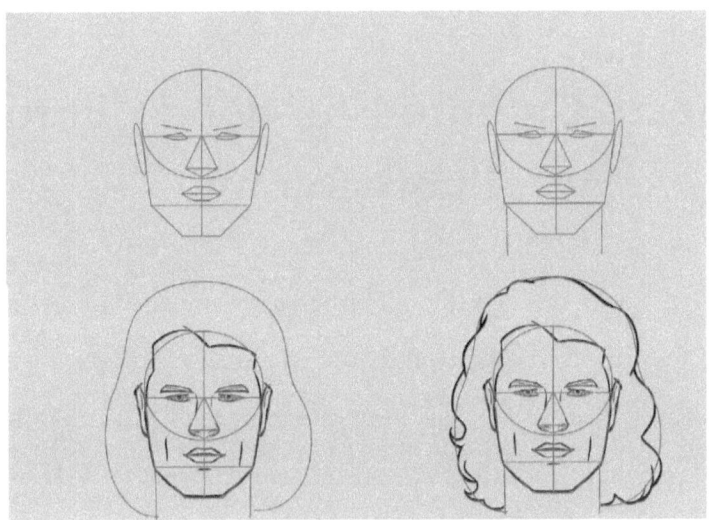

14. On the basis of the hair-guide, draw every detail of the hair.
15. Erase all sketchy guide lines.
16. Color the portrait with appropriate shades.

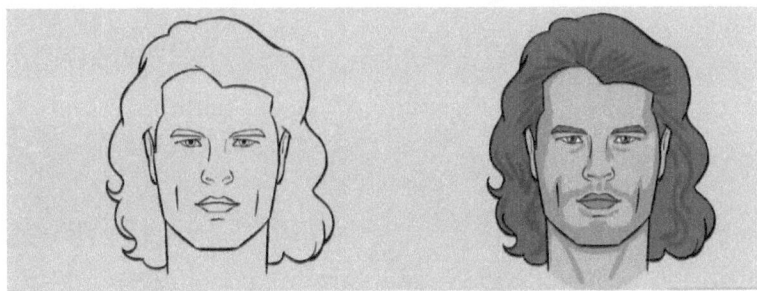

How to Capture Emotion in Portrait Photography

1. Position your subject

The environment can significantly maneuver our moods. As such, it's essential that photographers take time to consider the setting in which they capture their shot. Ask your subject questions that stimulate emotion, get them to move around or grab an object nearby to add to the shot.

More importantly, let them incorporate their own ideas as to how to best interact with the surroundings. This will enable them to also feel involved and in control of the shoot, rather than just a model subject to prearranged poses and ungenuine facial expressions.

In this shot, my daughter is strumming a guitar with her eyes closed as if performing at a concert. I had simply chosen a spot with great sunlight, and left the emotional unleashing all to this two-and-a-half-year-old. The result is, obviously, precious.

Portrait for Kids

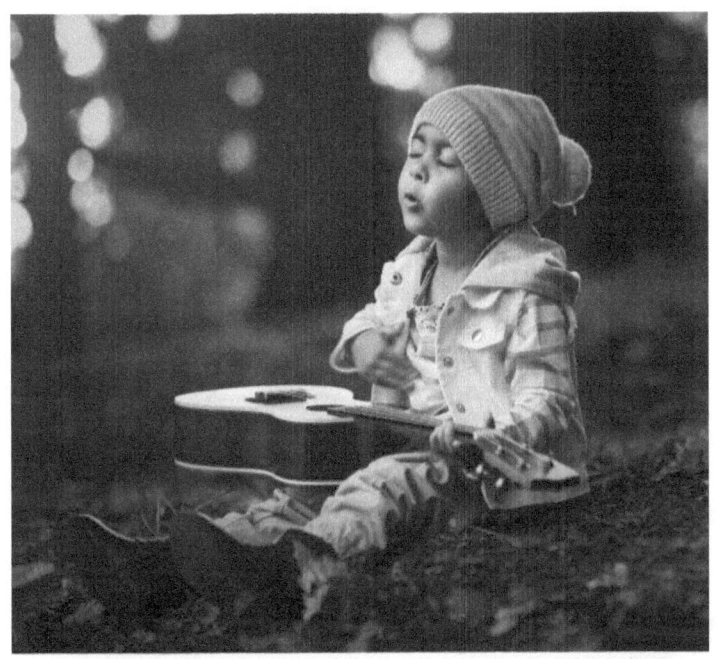

2. Lighting is important

Since your subject is your only channel of emotional expression, it is crucial that their face stands out visually. You can always rely on natural lighting to do the job, as long as your subject is facing the light source. In these instances, you would be able to use a low ISO of about 200. This would reduce most of the image's noise, leaving your subject's face with a smooth, detailed and clear surface.

The shot below was taken at a temple in Bali. The midday lighting and the temple's darkness created a perfect combination that set the image's tone. Of course, the ultimate embellishment was our little model's smile, and a dinner invitation from her family whom I had inadvertently befriended.

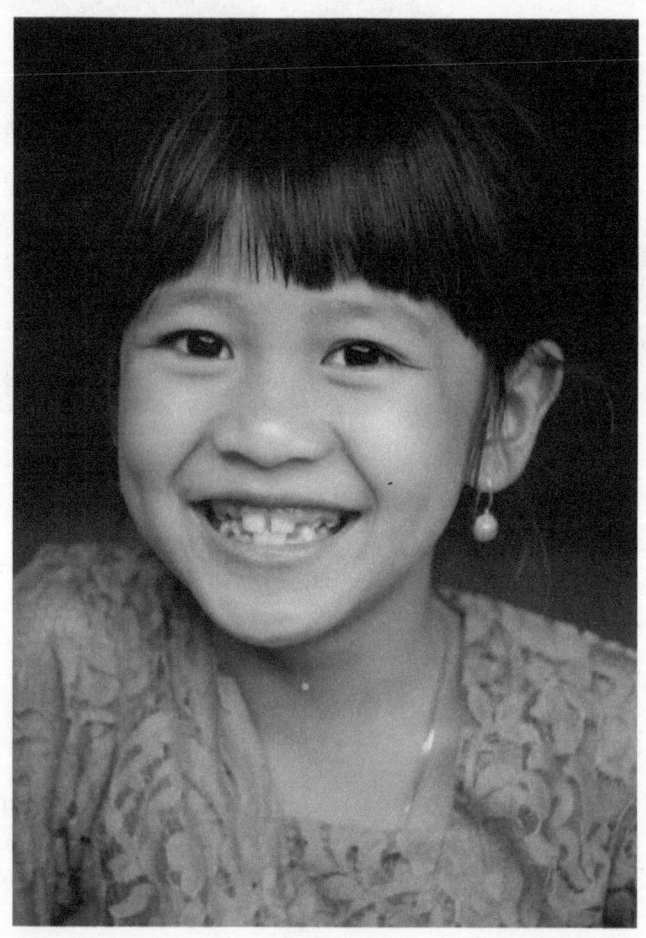

Portrait for Kids

3. The focus is on them

A photo showing provocative emotion is capable of telling profound stories. As a photographer, you should ensure the viewer is intrigued by nothing but your subject. This is when depth of field comes into play, whereby the image background is moderately blurred so that the main subject has exclusive focus.

A wide aperture gives an ideal depth of field regardless of your subject's distance from you, while ensuring details in the background are still visible. The two images below are taken with the Fujinon XF 90mm F/2. To balance out the large amount of light absorbed through the wide aperture, it is best to choose a fast shutter speed of around 1/400 sec. This also helps avoid shakiness and maintains details of your subject's face.

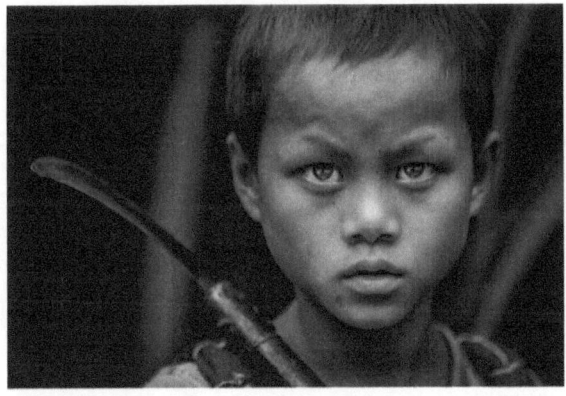

Portrait for Kids

In these shots, I gave the boys free reign to pose as they liked. The boy in the first image just managed to lift his sickle, creating a contrast against the looming bamboo leaves behind. The boy in the next image stood much further away. Yet with a large aperture and his confidence on camera, he remained just as clear and focused.

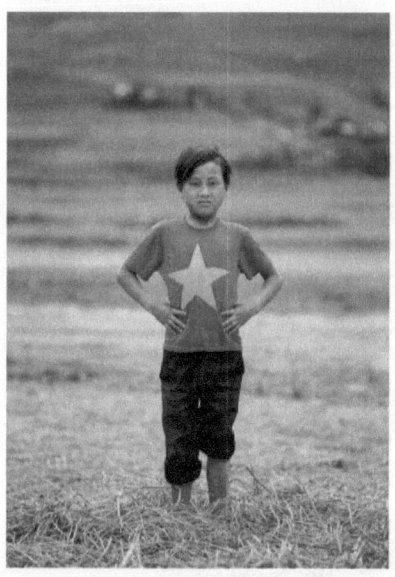

4. The right equipment goes a long way

Soft skills combined with the correct camera gear will help you make the most out of a photograph. Human portrait is about capturing powerful human expression while maintaining a high-quality image standard. My personal pick would be the FUJIFILM X100F with its 23mm F/2 prime lens, providing me with an impressive field of view.

Portrait for Kids

With its lightweight body, you can also move around freely while capturing the unique traits and manners of your subject.

I stumbled upon this boy in a market in Vietnam. Thanks to the broken rooftop, a ray of light landed on him just at the right moment. The result? It happened to be one of my most powerful shots.

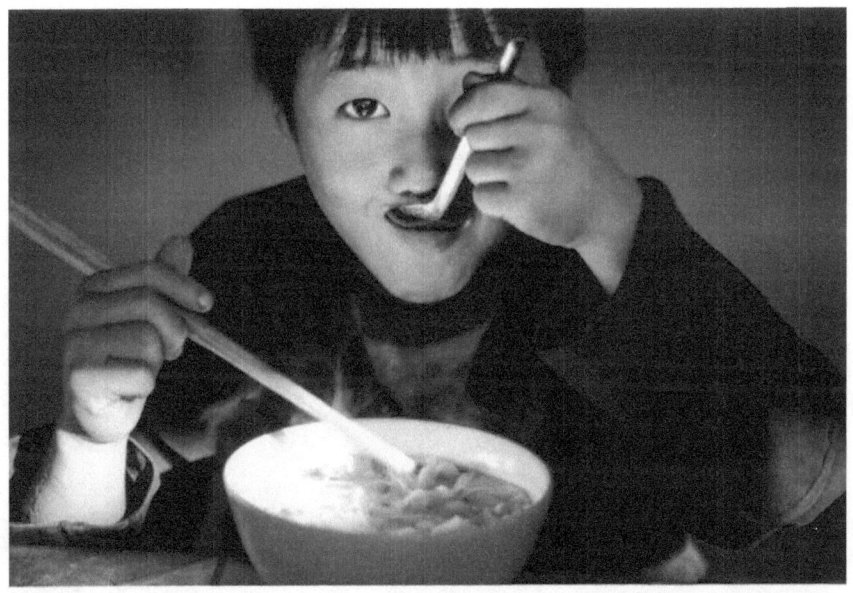

Portrait for Kids

Photographers have a special skill

1 – Get the mask to drop

There are things people want you to know about them, and things they don't. This is the mask worn every day by most of us to hide our inner selves. But you want emotion! you want character and feeling! you want to capture interesting moments!

The most honest portraits will often come when you get the mask to drop – and usually, it only takes a few minutes. People can only hold up the mask for so long.

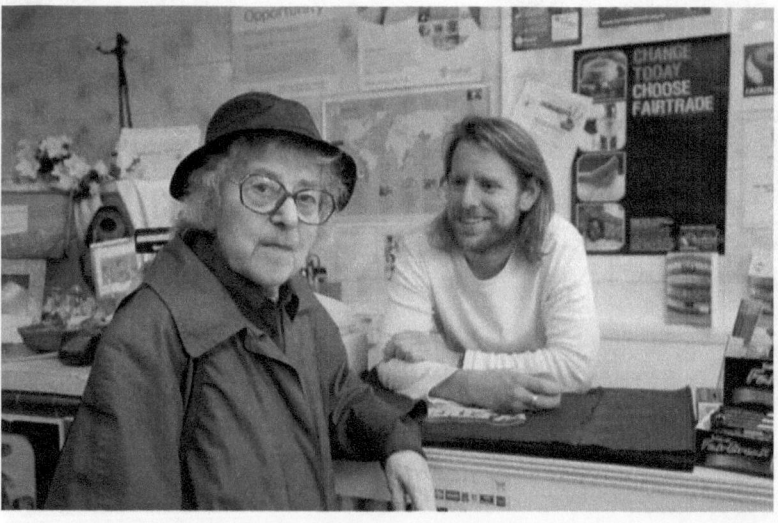

So once the mask drops you'll get flashes and moments where true feeling and thoughts come through. The inner world of your subject will be revealed. That will make for a way more interesting portrait –

Portrait for Kids

because when you capture emotion, your portrait will end up transmitting that emotion to the viewer.

Photography for me is not looking, it's feeling. If you can't feel what you're looking at, then you're never going to get others to feel anything when they look at your pictures. – Don McCullin

2 – Connect with your subject
A portrait is not made in the camera but on either side of it. – Edward Steichen.

The work of the photographer is done not by the camera but by the person who is taking the photo together with the subject. Your connection, the way they feel about you, will translate immediately into your images.

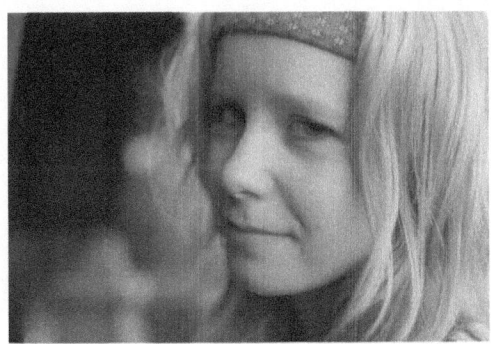

Portrait for Kids

Casual chit-chat helps to relax people. So that's what photographing a subject.

you never talk about the shot, just shoot the breeze, ask questions, talk about the day, the weather – it doesn't matter. It's just an opportunity to help them feel that this unnatural situation of them standing in front of me and my camera is totally natural.

always aim to have fun when shooting, not just because it elevates my mood, but also that of my subject.

3 – Or just lift your camera and see what happens
you don't always do the chit chat. Sometimes just pointing a camera at someone and seeing what happens results in awesome shots. Spontaneity counts for something!

The photo above was shot in this way and it's one of my favorite portraits. You can see that the woman's reaction is amused, and her posture is relaxed. The man, on the other hand, looks a bit annoyed, is more guarded. It's a nice contrast.

Portrait for Kids

People will react in wildly different ways when you photograph them unexpectedly – maybe they immediately button up or laugh nervously, start to pose, or react in an annoyed fashion.

4 – Let them peel the layers

Faces always talk too much. One line and all their plans are revealed. – Floriano Martins

Sometimes, you also just like to photograph over a period of time, maybe five or 10 minutes or longer, and let the subject peel. This works nicely if the person is very aware of their best angle and does a super staged pose.

you shoot what they want to show me, then carry on. After a couple of minutes people will just forget what they are doing and become preoccupied with everything else in their day, their life, or my stunning conversation skills (ha!).

Then bang! You suddenly have something interesting.

5 – Think about your energy

The definition of a great picture is one that stays with you, one that you can't forget. It doesn't have to be technically good at all. – Steve

Portrait for Kids

McCurry

How you are with your subject will really affect how the subject responds to the camera. That sounds obvious, but I've seen so many photographers wrapped up in their own nerves, who jump into taking someone's portrait and they don't get the shot because they are too wrapped up in themselves and their own thoughts. That burning desire to "get the shot!"

Become accustomed to really, really paying attention. That means leaving your own thoughts and feelings at the door. Be acutely aware of your subject! See who they are and what they are doing.

Remember that every part of the body reveals something – hands, posture, everything; you don't have to simply focus on the face.

6 – Use your instincts

There is so much being said by a person that goes beyond their bodies and what they do with it. The energy, the mood, the feelings, all play a part in what the person is saying about themselves. And trust me we are all saying a lot about ourselves that we aren't even aware of.

Use your instincts to get more information about how your subject is thinking and feeling – are their eyes sad but their face is attempting a smile? Are they acting shy but their eyes are burning with joy in the attention? Perhaps what they are really looking for is a nudge of reassurance from you and they'll really relax and enjoy themselves in from of the camera.

There are so many possibilities of how people think and feel. Learn to read people beyond their words and their immediate reactions. Ask yourself, what is going on for this person right now? How are they feeling? Bored, distracted, uncomfortable, excited?

7 – Be watchful and be present

If you wait, people will forget your camera, and the soul will drift up into view. – Steve McCurry

Being a watchful person is crazy useful in photography. Be happy to just wait, look, see, and ponder. Think Zen monk energy! By being present you are like the calm in the middle of a storm. You'll find most people are rushing around you, fidgeting, moving, sorting things out. Be calm and watchful and you'll start to see and notice so much more.

8 – Photograph what excites you!

It must move you! If it doesn't excite you, this thing that you see, why in the world would it excite me? – Jay Maisel

The best subjects are ones that you are totally fascinated by. Not just the ones who let you take their photo (although practice on those people for sure).

Be led by what you love. Have fun and have an awesome time – and that feeling and mood will ooze out of your photos.

9 – Look at the eyes

You don't have to sort of enhance reality. There is nothing stranger than truth. – Annie Leibovitz

The eyes can reveal some incredibly strong emotions. It's not always this way. All parts of the body play their part, but I love to look at someone, look into their eyes and see what happens.

People rarely look into each other's eyes for long, it's too powerful. So to capture someone in an image where they are really looking at the camera is fantastic.

Study the following images and see the different emotions conveyed through the eyes of the subjects.

Shading Techniques

Shading Techniques for Drawing

Techniques used for applying shading to an object are quite varied. Each technique produces a different texture and "feel" to the drawing. The drawing medium used may determine the shading technique that is applied in the drawing.

The most common application techniques include:

Hatching - Lines drawn in the same direction. By drawing lines closer together, darker values are created. Leaving more space between lines results in lighter values. For rounded objects, the lines may curve slightly around the form - following the contours of the object.

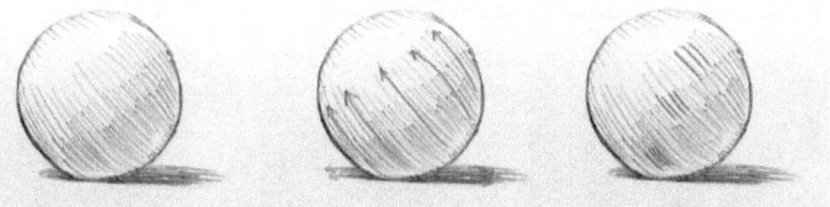

Cross-Hatching - Lines cross over each other. The density at which the lines cross over each other determines the value that is produced.

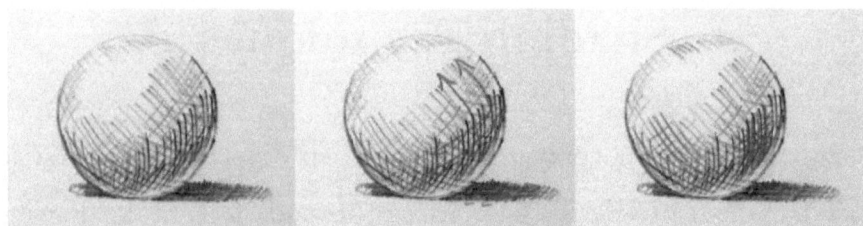

Blending - Smooth gradations of value are produced either by adjusting the amount of pressure applied to the medium or by using a blending tool, such a blending stump.

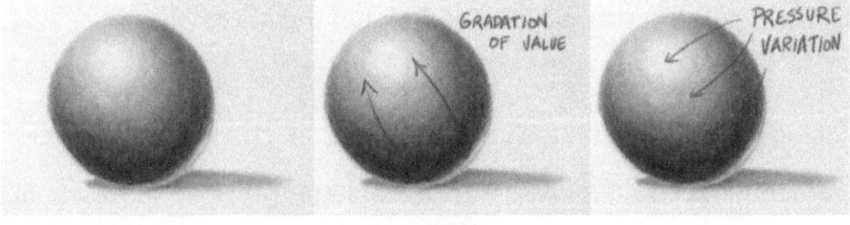

Rendering - Using an eraser to remove the medium to produce lighter values. This technique is typically used in conjunction with blending.

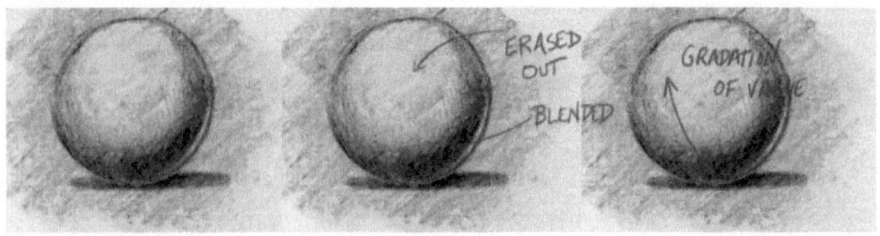

Random lines - Loose applications of crossing lines. The frequency in which the lines cross over each other determines the value produced.

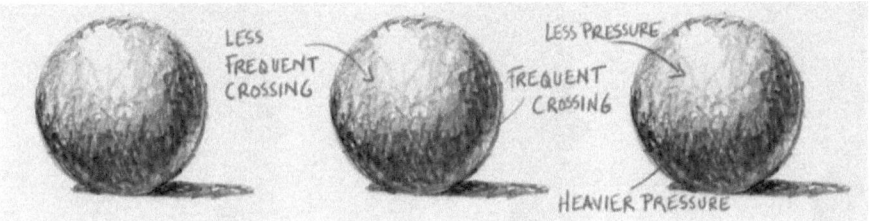

Stippling - Applying countless small dots to build up darker values in a drawing. The density of the dots determines the value produced.

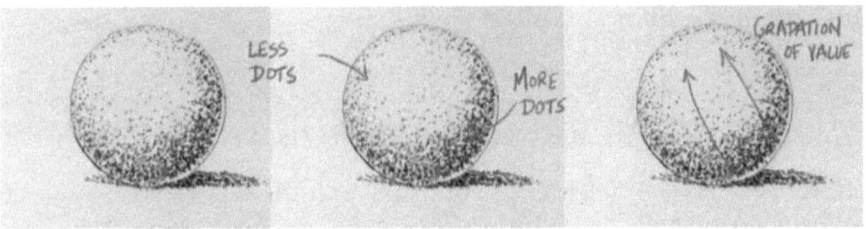

The Illusion of Light

It's easy to get caught up in the technique in which the material is applied and loose sight of the reason why we apply shading in the first place.

Light is how we see, after all, and shading informs us of the light within a scene. We understand the light within the scene through the use of value and contrast.

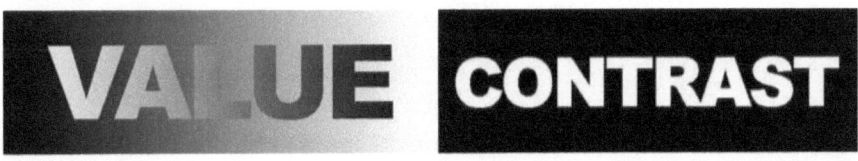

Value and contrast

Value is the darkness or lightness of a color. Light values are called tints and dark values are called shades.

Contrast deals with difference. Contrast is produced when any difference between elements such as texture, color, size, or value occurs. It can be subtle or extreme. When it comes to shading, we are mostly concerned with the contrast that is produced from changes in value.

When light hits the subject, it produces a range of contrasting values. The intensity of the light determines the contrast of values. Generally, the stronger the light - the higher the contrast.

Portrait for Kids

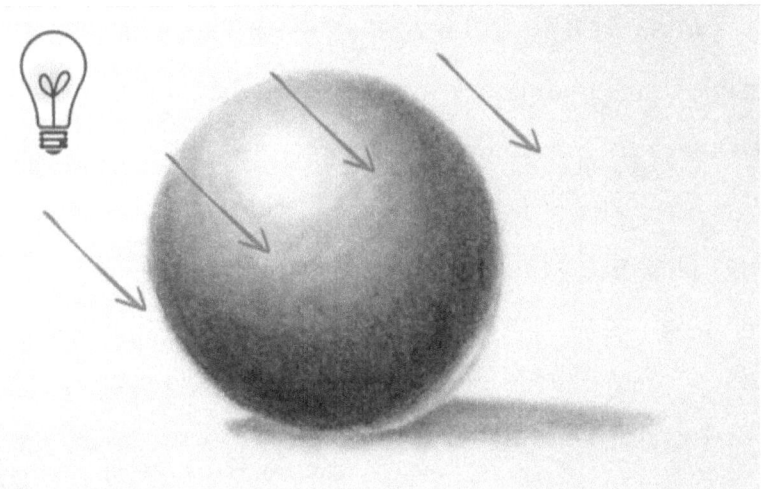

Values are arranged on the subject according to the location and intensity of the light source (or sources). To simplify the manner in which light behaves on a subject and surrounding objects, we'll look at what happens with just one light source on a smooth surface.

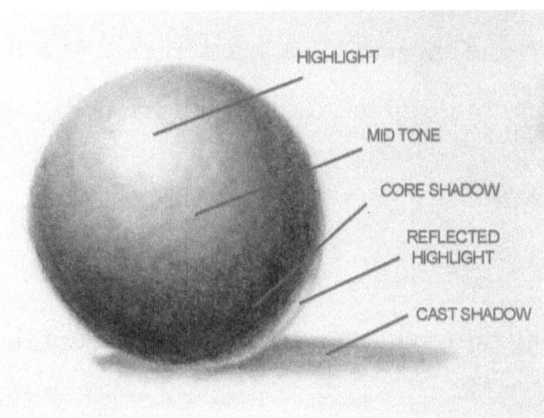

The locations of each area of value on the subject tell the viewer about the location of light and how the light behaves on the subject. The behavior of light (or how it is reflected) on the subject informs us about the texture and form of the subject.

Pencil Drawing- The Guide to Graphite
Take your pencil drawings to the next level. Learn how to master the medium of graphite in this comprehensive video course.

Locations of Value:

Highlight - The highlight is the location on the subject where the reflection of light is most intense. Highlights are typically indicated by a very light value of the color or in some cases - white.

Mid Tone - Mid tones are areas on the subject where some light is hitting, but in a manner that is less intense than the highlight. In many cases, the mid tone is the actual color (local color) or value of the subject.

Core Shadow - The core shadow is the area on the subject where light is prevented from hitting, producing an area of shadow. Core shadows are typically darker values of the local color.

Cast Shadow - Cast shadows are locations of darker value that result on surrounding objects or surfaces. Light is blocked from reaching these areas completely because another object is reflecting much of the light away.

Some light is reflected back off of surrounding objects and surfaces. This light bounces back onto objects producing an area of lighter value.

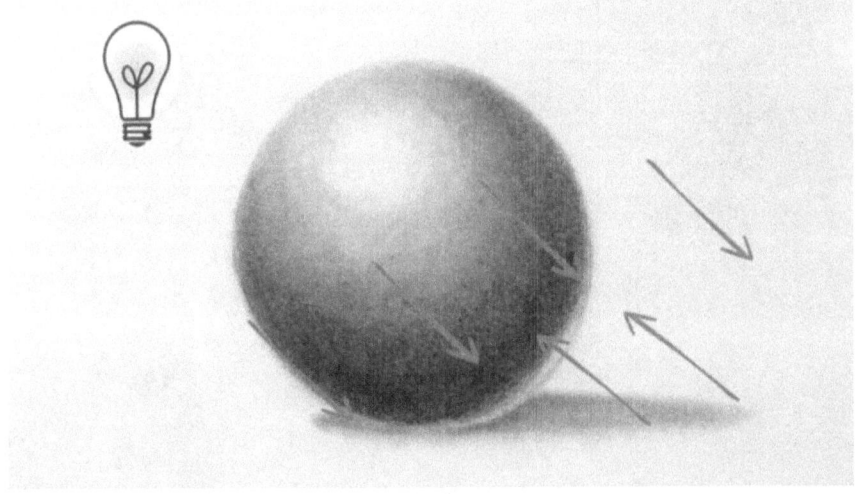

This area of slightly lighter value is referred to as a reflected highlight.

How to Shade Forms

As mentioned before, shading also informs the viewer of the form of the object. With a sphere, the change in value is gradual (gradation). Value becomes darker or lighter, depending on the lighting conditions. The same is true for other curved forms such as cones or cylinders.

For objects with flat sides (i.e. cube), the value stays fairly consistent for each side without much gradation. Each side of the cube may be a different value representing the highlight, mid tone, or core shadow.

But what about objects that have flat sides or planes that aren't cubes?

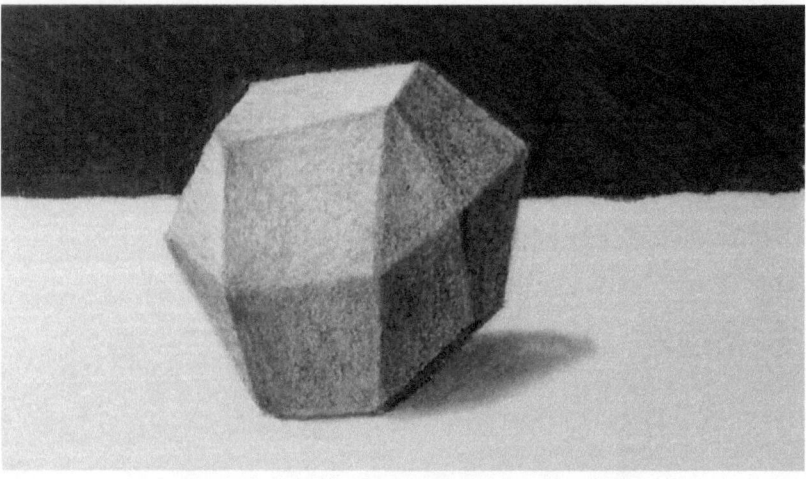

It is these situations where contrast plays an especially important role.

When shading, our goal is to depict the illusion of form and light. In most situations, this requires adding a full range of value. By comparing contrasting areas, we can evaluate the value in the drawing and make adjustments as necessary.

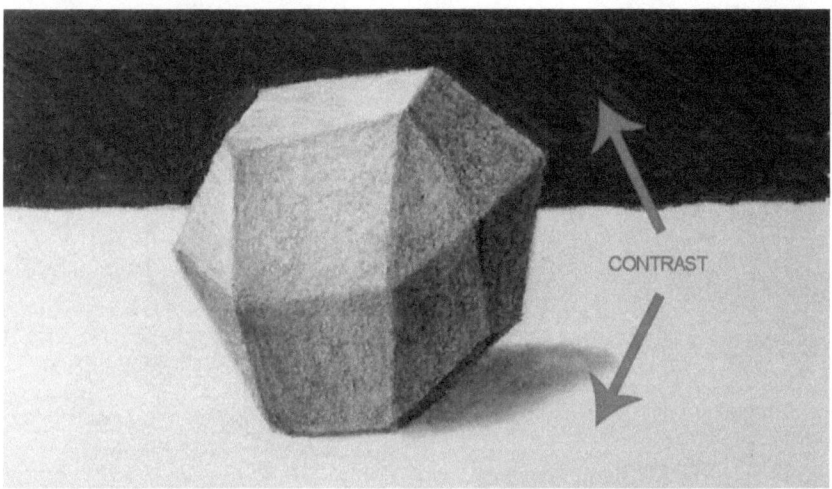

During the drawing process, a dark background is added. Adjustments to the values on the subject are made according to the contrast of values in the background and the table. Comparisons are made and the values are "pushed" in order to create a full range.

We can also exploit contrast to create edges and define the planes of the irregular form. By making the edges of each plane that are closer to the light source "a touch" lighter, we increase the contrast in value between each plane.

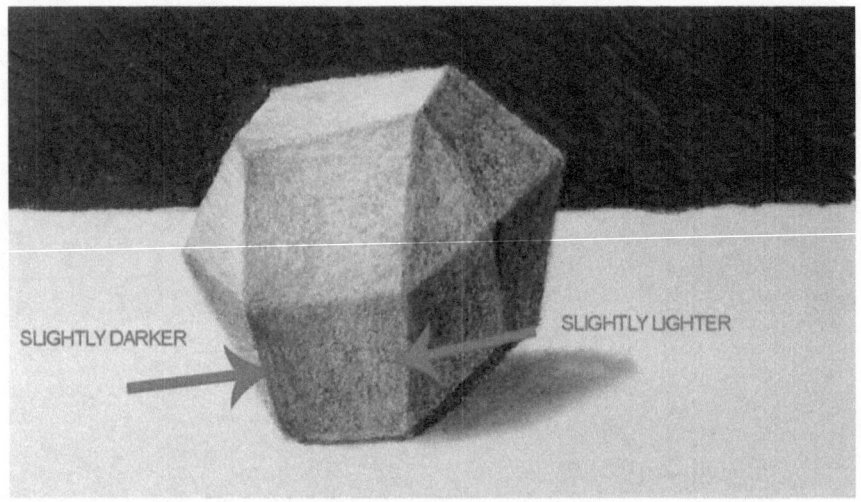

How to Shade Hollow Forms

Many objects are hollow or have recesses. To address objects such as these, we simply consider the direction of light, thinking of it as a line.

If light is coming from a certain direction, then it should continue until it hits an object. If the object is hollow, then the light will enter into the recess, producing an area of lighter value inside of it. Shadows are created on the opposite side of the edge of the recess, closest to the light source.

Portrait for Kids

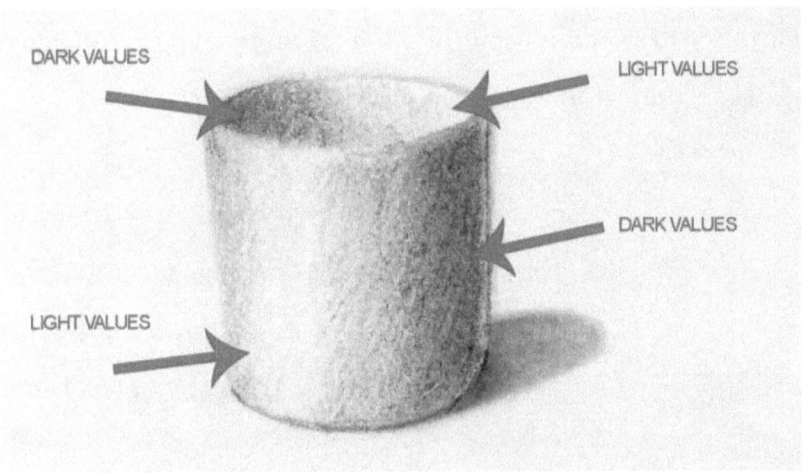

The outside of the hollow form is addressed as normal, with shadows further from the light source and highlights close to it.

Controlling the Medium
No matter which medium that you use to apply shading, control over the value produced is of paramount importance. The good news is that control over the medium simply requires patience and practice.

Once you have a clear understanding of how light behaves and how you can communicate it to the viewer, then you are already "half-way" there.

Practice drawing a few basic forms - a sphere, cube, and pyramid.

Shade them to communicate one light source using a full range of value. (Use contrast to make comparisons).

Once you have mastered these basic forms, move on to irregular forms and simple still life objects like apples or bananas. Look for the highlights, mid tones, core shadows, cast shadows, and reflected highlights. The more that you practice, the stronger you will become!

Portrait for Kids

Techniques For Highlighting

he first key to shading is knowing how to achieve different effects.

1. You can shade using pencils of different hardness or different mediums. Since H pencils are harder than B pencils, one technique for shading is to lay in different tones with different graphite pencils. This technique will result in a more textured look than blending tones from dark to light to produce shadow and highlighted areas. Charcoal and carbon pencils produce much darker tones than even soft graphite pencils, and may also be used in dark shadow areas, but because graphite is so slippery, charcoal will not layer over the top of it easily. It does work, however, to lay graphite over the top of charcoal.

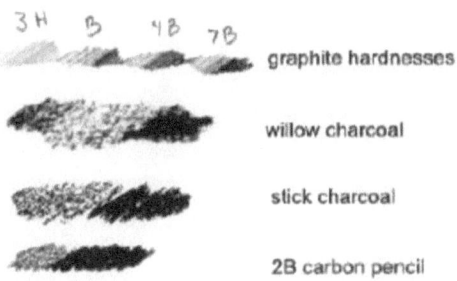

graphite hardnesses

willow charcoal

stick charcoal

2B carbon pencil

2. A second method for shading is to soften tones with a blending tool. Experiment with a a paper stump or tortillion, felt or

chamois cloth, tissue, other paper, q-tip, etc. Different tools produce different results, so use them accordingly; for instance, chamois cloth produces a very smooth finish that could be used for flesh, while using paper or tissue creates a more textured, uneven look that may compliment more roughly textured areas in the drawing.

3. Rubbing the pencil over the top of a texture or shape is a third way to render objects or create textures in drawings. Flat surfaces rubbed with the broad side of a stick of graphite or charcoal work best (such as wood, or raised metallic surfaces), and after the rubbing is complete, you can blend the texture with a blending tool and soften with a kneaded eraser to soften the form.

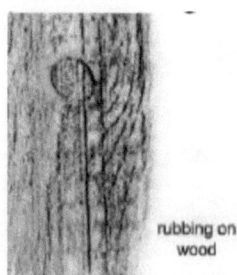
rubbing on wood

4. Highlights can be created in one of four ways: avoiding the light areas by shading around them, erasing after the fact (either by blotting areas with a kneaded eraser or by rubbing away lines and tone), masking off whites using masking tape or frisket film, or

Portrait for Kids

pressing into the paper with another tool and then rubbing over the top. A good way of achieving the last effect is to place tracing paper over the drawing so you can see where the lights will go, drawing the lines that are to remain white hard with a sharp pencil, and then removing the tracing paper and lightly shading over the pressed lines. If you use tape on your paper, reduce the stickiness by pressing it against your clothes first, and practice lifting it off a scrap of the same paper before trying it on your drawing.

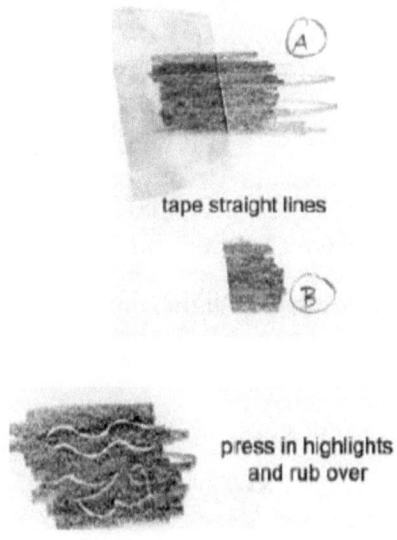

tape straight lines

press in highlights
and rub over

How to Take a Good Selfie

1. Lighting is Everything

It sounds obvious, but the first rule of selfie-ing is to pay attention to your lighting. You need good lighting. Natural lighting. As vlogger Jordan Liberty puts it, "Light is undoubtedly the best beauty product you don't have to pay for." Instead of facing your computer screen or television, turn toward a window with natural light. Or better yet, go outside and bask in the sun's glow (with sunscreen on). Good lighting can actually make undereye circles and shadows totally disappear.

If you're shooting your selfie inside, beauty blogger (and frequent selfie-taker) Michelle Phan advises that you find a window. "Having nice, natural sunlight streaming in will make for a good selfie. Another thing do is take a piece of white paper and hold it underneath my chin, which creates a natural bounce of light, illuminates the face, and also reduces the double-chin effect."

2. Avoid Shadows

"There is nothing worse than having a huge shadow cast over your face," says photographer and style blogger Candice Lake. "When in doubt, face directly into or away from the sun. If it's the middle of the day and the sun is high, the shadows can look like bags under your eyes. The golden hour to shoot a photo is during sunrise or sunset, when the light is low and the most beautiful."

3. Know When to Use Flash

While finding natural light and avoiding shadows are key tips to how to take a good selfie, there are times when you want to take a selfie and it's dark. Whether you're in the club or just on your couch watching Netflix, how do you get a great selfie in little to no light? Turn to Snapchat. The app has a flash feature for the front-facing camera, while the regular photo app on iPhone does not. In Snapchat, hit the little lightning bolt on the top left corner and then take your selfie. The screen will burst bright white light on your face. It won't look perfect by any means (it gives the photo a subtle blue cast), but at least you'll be able to see your face. Once you save it to your camera roll, you can play with the tone to make it a little less blue.

4. Smile Like You Mean It

"Flash a real smile and no image will look bad," says Lake. Don't contort your face into a grin that's too big or forced. Natural smiles are always better. On the other hand, if you're going for slightly more serious selfie, pull a Tyra and "try smiling with your eyes." Lake's advice for perfecting the smize? Practice in front of the mirror until you get it right. You'll get the hang of it!

5. Take a Lot of Selfies...and We Mean A LOT

Kylie Jenner's best selfie tip is just to take selfies. A lot of selfies. She's said that she takes "like, 500 selfies" before she finds one she likes enough to post. "Sometimes regret putting one up if find a better one later. like damn, that's a better photo, but that's the only thing regret," she has said. Try tilting your head in different directions and changing the angles up slightly between each shot so there's a wide variety to choose from. And don't forget to make sure the camera's focused before snapping away.

You can film your selfie session instead of taking standard pictures. Press record on the video option instead and pose away. After a minute or two of this, you can scroll through the video and freeze a frame with the best selfie. It sounds silly, but you can actually pull out the best selfie poses this way (and no one will ever know the difference!).

Portrait for Kids

6. Play to Your Angles

If there's one piece of advice you should take from Kim Kardashian, it's this: When it comes to selfies, keep your chin down and the camera up. There are about five people in the world who look good when shot from under their chin, and we haven't met any of them. When taking a selfie, hold the phone so that the bottom of it is level with your eyes. Or better yet, use a selfie stick. They're ridiculous in every way except one: Because you hold them up high, they make everyone look svelte and supermodel-y in photos.

Furthermore, you probably shouldn't stare directly into the camera. "Most people don't look their best straight-on. Turn to the side a little bit — not to the point where it's a full-on profile, but just slightly," says makeup artist Nick Barose.

7. Use the Right Apps and Filters
"you have a soft spot for the Valencia [Instagram] filter. It's the dreamiest of all filters and it makes everyone look gorgeous," says Lake, who also recommends the Afterlight app for editing camera-

phone photos. If you're really serious about selfies, Phan recommends the Samsung Galaxy S5 phone, which has a selfie mode. "It makes everything easy. I take a picture and it automatically airbrushes my face and it brightens it," she says. There's no shame in editing a photo of yourself before posting it to the 'Gram. We also love Facetune, which lets you subtly blur, shape, morph, and define certain areas of your face. Blogger Amanda Steele likes the filters on VSCO, but other great apps are Perfect365 and Adobe Photoshop Fix. Don't like your under-eye bags? Blur them away! Want to whiten your teeth? Go for it. A subtle trick on Facetune is to "detail" your eyes, which makes them look bright and sparkly. What's on the Internet lives forever, after all.

8. Don't Over-Edit

While we're all for editing and filtering, don't adjust your selfie to the point that it looks unnatural. When editing, use a really light touch. It's easy to get carried away. Only touch up the areas that are glaringly obvious to you — those little lines around your eyes make you look human. If you're using a filter, you also have the option to not use it at max capacity. Instead of just selecting a photo filter on Instagram, click on the filter itself (Amaro, Valencia, etc.) until a sliding bar comes up. Then you can reduce the severity of the filter, making the photo appear

Portrait for Kids

a little less edited.

9. Be Mindful of Your Background

The best selfies have either interesting backgrounds (Oh, you're just casually selfie-ing while skydiving? Great.) or really, really simple ones. The middle ground is what's deadly. And beware of photo-bombers.

10. Don't Overthink It

Just relax. A trying-too-hard selfie is never going to be a good one. "The thing about selfies is that you don't want them to be too serious. If your makeup looks like it took you an hour to do and you look too posed, you're not doing it right," says Barose. The best selfie poses are the ones that come naturally to you.

11. Avoid Cliché Selfies

Rule of thumb: If it looks like something a teenager on MySpace circa 2004 would have done, you shouldn't be doing it. "No one needs to do that Kim Kardashian duck-lips face," says Barose. It might give you killer cheekbones — but it's time to retire it.

Should you find yourself overwhelmed by the urge to throw up some sort of faux gang sign...put down your iPhone and do not let yourself near any other camera until the urge subsides. Most of the time, people rely on those poses because they feel uncomfortable. But Lake has a trick for loosening up: "If you feel a little stiff, walk away and then step into the frame again and snap quickly. You'll have less time to be self-conscious."

12. Embrace Natural Expressions
"Right before you snap a selfie, say 'yes' in your head, or 'yasss' if you're feeling extra sassy. You can also inhale just as you hit the shutter for lightly parted lips and a relaxed expression," Liberty says. He also recommends keeping your eyes shut until the moment before you take the shot. "Expressions look best when they're fresh."

Creative Self Portrait Ideas for Photographers

10. Pretend You're in a Movie (My Favourite One!)

If you are like me and you love cinematic portraits, you'll enjoy acting in front of the camera. Create a story in your mind, visualise the scenes, and recreate them through self-portrait photography.

Your idea doesn't need to have a complicated twist or a surprising ending. In the editing process, add two black lines above and below your photos. You can even crop them, so they look more like film stills.

Doing this is a great reason to rewatch films to get even more inspiration for future projects.

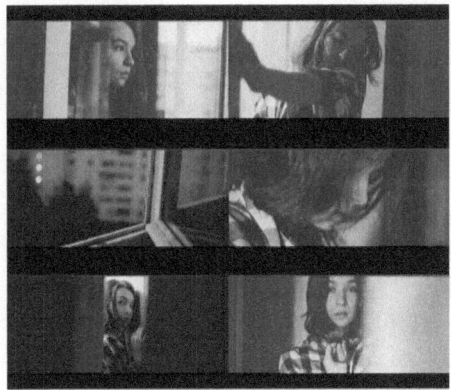

Portrait for Kids

9. Convert Your Self Portraits to Black & White To Make them Even More Interesting

Black and white portraits are a special genre of their own. If there's an emotion you'd like to emphasise, experiment with B&W photography.

It will highlight your feelings and add texture to details you would ignore. It also gives you more experience in the genre.

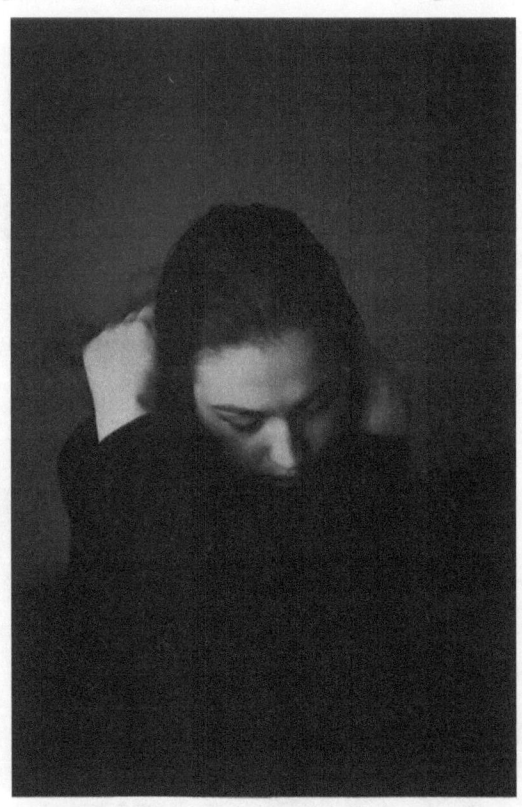

Portrait for Kids

8. Take Photos in a Limited Space

Having too many options at once can feel paralysing. Limiting yourself by shooting at only one location can improve your work.

Do a photoshoot in one room and try to make the pictures look as if you took them in different locations.

It will not only give you a fun project to work on but force you to look at your surroundings from a new perspective. This challenge will also make you focus on details that you usually overlook.

It will improve your general creativity and sharpen your ability to notice great things in simple places. What you learn during this process will come in handy in every future shoot.

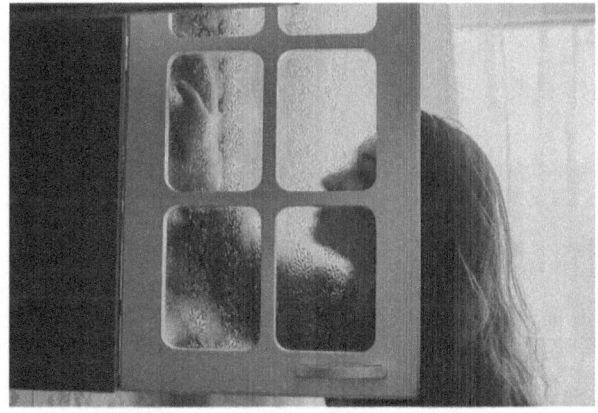

7. Take Photos with Your Pet (Or a Person!)

Pets are photogenic, so why not include them in your photos? If you own a pet or live next to someone who means a lot to you, take a photo with them.

Getting support during a self-portrait photography session will give you comfort, warmth, and lots of ideas. It will also strengthen the bond you have with your loved one.

If your pet doesn't enjoy sitting still, don't force it. Experiment, be silly and don't be afraid of making mistakes. Experimental photos end up being the best ones, anyway.

6. Take Two Photos and Make a Diptych

A diptych is a "collage" made of two photos. These images often contain many subjects that tell a detailed story about the photographer. This is particularly handy in self-portraiture.

You can combine a simple photo of yourself with a gorgeous photo of nature. Diptychs come in handy when you have two photos you like a lot. Instead of having to choose one, you can use them both at once!

Portrait for Kids

Self portrait photography of a dark haired girl using two pictures to make a diptych.

5. Stick to One Colour at a Time

Pick a single colour and create a self-portrait photo series inspired by it. Though the photos don't have to feature one colour only, they should all have a similar colour scheme.

This project will refresh you, challenge your imagination, and give you a chance to unleash your creativity. Plus, you can base the photoshoot on the clothes in your wardrobe.

A girl poses for self portrait photography emphasising the use of only one colour, green

4. Experiment with Shadows and Lighting

My favourite portrait photographers are excellent at shadow-play. You can do so much with the help of a single light source and a pattern.

Give yourself as much freedom as possible when you experiment with light. Use sun hats, curtains, hands, plants, to create incredible, creative self-portrait photography.

Portrait for Kids

Light is a priceless tool that can make the simplest portraits look fantastic. When you become a master of light, you become a master of photography. Take photos both indoors and outdoors, and don't be afraid to break the rules as you do.

Don't be scared of working with artificial light. You don't need to invest in professional lighting equipment. You can use any indoor light you own to take creative self-portraits.

you often use a lamp to light my face because it lets me experiment with new angles and styles. you don't have to worry about time, which isn't the case when it comes to ever-changing natural light.

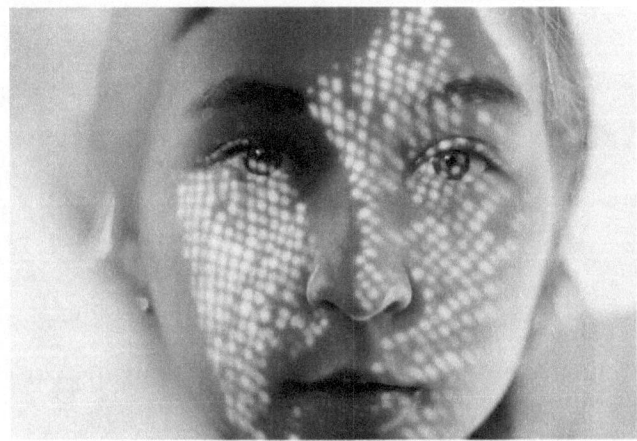

Portrait for Kids

3. Stitch a Few Photos to Make a Panoramic Self Portrait

Panoramas are fun to make and pleasant to look at. This is how I make mine:

First, using a tripod, I take vertical self-portraits that don't crop any of my limbs and leave some space around me.

Then, I go back to my camera and take photos of the areas I'd like to stitch. I make sure that I don't make any quick movements or position myself to another location.

After that, I import my photos into Lightroom. I select the photos I'd like to stitch, and go to Photo > Edit In > Merge to Panorama in Photoshop.

Finally, I colour correct the results.

A self portrait picture of a redheaded woman standing on a road.

2. Document the Seasons

Each season has something worth photographing. Take self-portraits every season. This way, you can work on a year-long project. The results will give you pleasant memories, show you every side of nature's beauty, and impress others.

Portrait for Kids

If a long-term project doesn't excite you, make the most of the current season. Think of what you like about it. It could be the blooming sunflowers of summer or the colourful fallen leaves of autumn.

Photograph that and include yourself in it.

1. Recreate Your Favourite Story

Do you have a favourite film, book, or painting that inspires you? Recreate it! My favourite forest and Little Red Riding Hood inspired the photo below. All I needed was a simple red cloak and a fitting location.

Recreating stories is an excellent opportunity to dive into a new world and find new ideas.

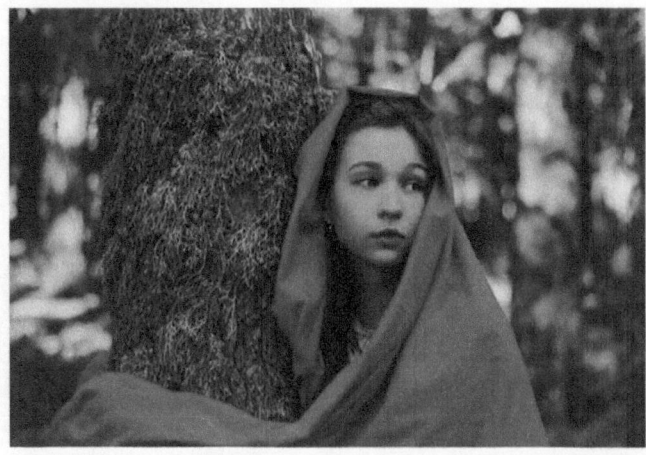

www.ingramcontent.com/pod-product-compliance
Lightning Source LLC
Chambersburg PA
CBHW030508220526
45464CB00006B/2711